Monday Morning Jesus

*Turning Your Retreat
into Everyday Living*

Joseph Moore

*illustrations by
Tom Cirone*

Paulist Press ◇ **New York/Ramsey**

Library of Congress
Catalog Card Number: 83-61997

ISBN: 0-8091-2591-9

Published by Paulist Press
545 Island Road, Ramsey, New Jersey 07446

Printed and bound in the
United States of America

Contents

◇ *Acknowledgements*

I would like to thank Peter Ferreira, Patti Sullivan and Patrick Brown, O.C.S.O. for sharing their reflections with me.

Special thanks to my mentor on adolescence, Doug Fazzina.

Dedication

for my friend, Bob Loxley

Introduction

The title of this book refers to the experience of facing life the *day* after your retreat or weekend experience. It isn't easy, believe me. When you walk into the house eager to share your intense experience, you may find the members of your family somewhat uninterested. It's even possible that they will misunderstand you and feel negative about your experience. That's a real "downer."

Another difficulty can be going into school on Monday morning after the retreat and finding yourself thrust back, very abruptly, into the boring routine of every day. If there are friends at school who also experienced the retreat, it makes it *somewhat* easier to keep the experience alive. But maybe no one in your school was on the weekend. If this is the case, it could make you feel pretty lonely and isolated. And even if some of your classmates have shared in your experience you probably have other friends who have not—and that can cause problems too. The feeling of being alone after a retreat experience can be just as strong as the feeling of being together during the retreat.

And so it is that the title was given to this book. These feelings of being unappreciated, misunderstood, lonely, and isolated are normally to be expected at least to some degree. They are not totally bad feelings in themselves. In fact, they can be considered part of the total growth experience of the weekend. It is only when these feelings catch us totally unprepared and unexpected that they can really devastate us. It's only when we try to avoid these feelings or become unwilling to cope with them that they can cause us any emotional harm. The thing to do is to face the feelings head-on, usually with the help of others, and try to understand them so that we can come to the full maturity which the retreat experience has opened up for us.

After all, what is the meaning of the word "retreat"? It means to go away from, to back off our everyday busy lives and to go off to a special place for a little while. It means an opportunity to reflect, either alone or in a close group, upon this business of daily living and how we are doing at it. It is a time to examine our own inner souls and its deepest feelings. It's a time to think about and talk about who we *really* are inside. It's a time to meditate on our relationships with family and friends and of course with Jesus. It's a time to pray and get in touch with ourselves and others. It's a time to receive the healing touch of the affirmation of friends. It's a time to overcome in some small way our fears and anxieties and to attempt to trust ourselves and others and God's word. It's a time for growth and change and becoming the person we are meant to be.

However much needed and intense this retreat experience is, it must come to an end. Why? Because emotionally we cannot as human beings live at such a level of intensity for very long. Also because we have to get on with the business of daily living, of growing up and maturing, of reaching out and helping others. In fact, the purpose of the retreat is simply to help us to do a better job of living our daily lives, of facing Monday morning.

In the early days of the Church when people went on a retreat they left the city and went into the desert to fast and pray and think. And then they would return to the city, just as you return to your high school or college or place of work. They returned a little bit wiser, a little bit holier, a little bit more in touch with themselves, with other people, and with God. The purpose of this book is to help you through a variety of daily reflections over a period of two months so that you will come to fully understand your retreat experience and *all* the feelings and movements within you it has triggered (or the Holy Spirit has triggered). It is to help you to stretch yourself to grow as much as you possibly can from this tremendous spiritual opportunity which has been given to you. I hope you use it well.

Monday Morning Jesus

Week 1 ◇ Monday

You are probably pretty tired today—"wiped out" both emotionally and physically. But if your retreat was a good experience for you, you probably also have a real reserve of energy for love and for living. This is a wonderful thing, so rejoice in it. Bask in the feelings of self-worth you have recently experienced. Let yourself feel the warmth of the new levels of friendship you have achieved. Appreciate the closeness to Jesus that you have. You might even want to do a little daydreaming about the weekend today. But what is very important today is not that you pray and reflect but rather that you rest. When we are very tired it's almost impossible to pray (later in this book we will talk about the importance of good physical conditioning in relationship to prayerful life). So just be thankful today that you have another day of life and that will be a prayer enough.

To Do:

Take a nap or retire early.

Good News for Today:

Each day over these next months a short selection from the New Testament will be selected for you to think about. If you don't have a New Testament, try to pick one up for tomorrow.

Week 1 ◇ Tuesday

Being back at school or wherever is really hard right after a retreat because the intensity of that experience just cannot compare with the routine of daily life. If you haven't begun to feel the drudgery of the usual sweeping over you, you probably will experience it someday this week. And that's O.K. It is very normal. It is simply a feeling. It doesn't mean that there is anything wrong *either* with the retreat *or* with a daily routine. It just means that emotionally we require a transition time between intense experiences and less intense experiences. Sometimes that takes a little time. For most folks it takes a few days, but it is not abnormal for it to take a couple of weeks. So don't feel weird if it takes you a while to "readjust." Just be patient with yourself. It helps at least a little bit to talk about this transition with someone else who is either also going through it at the same time or else has been through it in the past. You can also talk to Jesus about the experience you are having. He understands every feeling we ever have.

To Do:

Talk to another person about how you are feeling today.

Good News for Today:

"But happy are your eyes because they see, your ears because they hear! I tell you solemnly, many prophets and holy men longed to see what you see, and never saw it; to hear what you hear, and never heard it." (Matthew 13:16–17)

Coming Down the Mountain
Week 1 ◇ Wednesday

When something wonderful or special has happened to us, a strong temptation we can have is to want to continue to indulge that experience beyond its limits. For example, we can want a wonderful trip or an excellent party or a good song to last forever. Sometimes we play an album over and over to help us stretch out an experience. There is nothing wrong with this normal tendency. But sometimes people who have been on a retreat never want the experience to end—which means they don't care to deal with that daily reality staring them in the face. There are various ways of prolonging the retreat experience. Some of them are healthy and some are not. One that isn't advisable is to make plans right away to go on a retreat again in the very near future. This isn't wise because first of all it means that you aren't allowing the most recent experience to really sink in. Secondly, to go on retreats with any frequency is to rob them of their real meaning and their specialness. Retreats are supposed to remove us from daily life, not become a part of it.

Of course it is great to feel that you would like to go on another retreat at some future time or aspire even to be part of a retreat team—but just not right away. Even Jesus' apostles had this temptation when they had the special experience of a vision called the "transfiguration." We have included it as your good news reflection for today.

To Do:

Try to put out of your mind this week the idea of your next retreat so that you won't get distracted from all the feelings still coming from your current experience.

Good News for Today:

"Six days later, Jesus took with him Peter and James and his brother John and led them up a high mountain where they could be alone. There in their presence he was transfigured: his face shone like the sun and his clothes became as white as the light. Suddenly Moses and Elijah appeared to them; they were talking with him. Then Peter spoke to Jesus. 'Lord,' he said, 'it is wonderful for us to be here; if you wish, I will make three tents here, one for you, one for Moses and one for Elijah.'" (Matthew 17:1–4)

Note:

Just as the apostles wanted to stay up on the mountain after this magnificent experience we can want to stay on our retreat. And yet Jesus brings his friends back down the mountain, back down from the experience to everyday life.

Community vs. Clique

Week 1 ◇ Thursday

One of the very important ways of continuing to nourish a retreat experience is to stay in touch with the other people who shared this growth experience. This isn't so that you can simply have fond memories together. No, it's in order to help you to *continue* to grow through mutual support. Maybe there are other kids in your school or parish who shared the retreat with you. This makes on-going support a lot easier. If there is no one in your immediate environment who also shared the retreat you can still stay in touch by letter writing, phone calls, and visits. It's helpful to stay in touch to some extent with the retreat community especially right after the weekend.

What we are talking about here is the need for a supportive community which all of us need to help us grow. We are not, however, talking about a clique. You would be forming a post-retreat clique if you chose only to associate with other retreatants and ignored all your former friends. And this can happen, sometimes not in very noticeable ways but in more subtle ways. A community is a group of people who bond together and stay close in order to grow and to open themselves for others outside their community. A clique is a close group which shuts itself off from those outside of it—and this is a deadening experience. Always remember that your retreat showed you the beautiful possibilities of openness and caring that exist within *all* people, not just the ones who were fortunate enough to share in the retreat with you. Your challenge is to help unlock that tremendous potential that lies within *all* people you know. And you can only unlock it if people still feel that you care about them even though they haven't shared in your retreat.

To Do:

Seek out a friend who was not on your retreat and ask him or her to share with you how *he* or *she* spent the weekend.

Good News for Today:

"His mother and brothers now arrived and, standing outside, sent in a message asking for him. A crowd was sitting around him at the time the message was passed to him, 'Your mother and brothers and sisters are outside asking for you.' He replied, 'Who are my mother and my brothers?' And looking around at those sitting in a circle about him, he said, 'Here are my mother and my brothers. Anyone who does the will of God, that person is my brother and sister and mother.' " (Mark 3:31–35)

The Undoing of Masks
—A Process

Another difficulty often encountered after a retreat is the realization that people tend to slip rather easily back into their old ways. A weekend can have a profound effect upon a person and even cause or begin some profound changes—but it doesn't remake the total personality. And so you may discover that somebody who was very warm and open with you on the retreat has slipped back into his or her old shyness or distancing or unfriendliness. When this happens it is very hard to take. First of all it can be hurtful to us. Secondly it can cause us to question the genuineness of that person during the weekend. If you feel that suspicion, try to dismiss it. Try to realize that such people probably were their true self on the retreat, that it was one special time when they felt secure enough to take off their false "front." But they obviously are not secure enough to keep the mask off, and so when they are thrust back into their daily environment they lack the inner strength to be themselves.

As difficult as it is if you turn away from them or if you label them as fakes, this is going to drive them deeper into their own insecurity. They may lose even the hope of being free again. Secretly, unconsciously even, they may be wondering if you, having gotten a glimpse of their true self, will support them enough so that they can recapture that experience. It also can be true that sometimes when we are upset with others because their behavior is not consistent with their behavior on the retreat, we are in fact more upset with ourselves. Realizing the inconsistency of our own words and actions and

8

YOU THINK WE SHOULD CHANGE OUR IMAGE SINCE WE'VE DECIDED TO FOLLOW JESUS?

experiencing the return to our old ways or our handy masks, we may prefer to direct that anger toward others. It's an old psychological truth that the things we don't like about ourselves are often the very same things we find hard to tolerate in others.

To Do:

Say a prayer to Jesus asking him to help you be patient with the growth process in others.

Good News for Today:

"Do not judge, and you will not be judged; because the judgments you give are the judgments you will get, and the amount you measure out is the amount you will be given. Why do you observe the splinter in your brother's eye and never notice the plank in your own? How dare you say to your brother, 'Let me take the splinter out of your eye,' when all the time there is a plank in your own? Hypocrite! Take the plank out of your own eye first, and then you will see clearly enough to take the splinter out of your brother's eye." (Matthew 7:1–5)

What Is Reality?

Week 1 ◊ Saturday

To conclude our week of meditations on the "post-retreat syndrome" let's talk about a little confusion which might also creep up on you. After getting some time and space from a retreat and after reacclimating to the daily routine one might be tempted to say: Which is reality—the retreat or normal life? What's real and unreal? Are kids their real selves or not on a retreat? Often these questions are the result of disappointment with ourselves, our friends, our society, that all does not continue to be as it was on the retreat. But can it? It seems unfair to label a retreat "unreal." In actual fact, a retreat is a very real experience. It provides an atmosphere where people feel freedom to be their true selves without the judgment of society. And as a result of individual openness the "society" on a retreat becomes itself a new and freeing experience. And if the retreat is to have an impact on your life, it is very important that you trust this experience as very real and true. The nuance or distinction that needs to be made is that the intensity of the retreat experience cannot be constantly sustained because we cannot always be focused on our relationships with ourselves, with others, and with God. Why not? Because we also have tasks to do in the world, the business of survival and daily living. Work (which probably for you is being a student) is necessary not only for the maintenance of the human community but for our own psychological health as well. In addition to work there is exercise and recreation and entertainment and rest and prayer—and so many other dimensions to human life. Going on a retreat is taking time out of daily life to focus on our feelings and spirituality. It is very real but it is a special time. The secret of making the retreat experience part of everyday reality is the constant struggle to be ourselves and love ourselves, to accept others, to be in touch with our feelings, to express our feelings, and to continue to pray. This struggle is the bridge that connects the retreat to "real life."

To Do:

Meditate on the good news today, comparing the physical disappearance of Jesus and how it made his friends feel to your own departure from the retreat weekend and how it is making you feel.

Good News for Today:

"Now having met together, they asked him, 'Lord, has the time come? Are you going to restore the kingdom to Israel?' He replied, 'It is not for you to know times or dates that the Father has decided by his own authority, but you will receive power when the Holy Spirit comes on you, and then you will be my witnesses not only in Jerusalem but throughout Judaea and Samaria, and indeed to the ends of the earth.'

As he said this he was lifted up while they looked on, and a cloud took him from their sight. They were still staring into the sky when suddenly two men in white were standing near them and they said, 'Why are you men from Galilee standing here looking into the sky? Jesus who has been taken up from you into heaven, this same Jesus will come back in the same way as you have seen him go there.'" (Acts 1:6–11)

════ A Definition of Spirituality

Week 2 ◊ Sunday

There is a word thrown around a great deal these days. That word is "spirituality." It is confusing to use because while our understanding of its meaning has dramatically shifted we continue to use the word. We've done the same thing with the word "retreat." Older people may tell you that retreats to them mean going away from the busy world in order to be alone in silent prayer with God. For the younger generation a retreat means going away from the busy world to become intimately close to other people in deep personal sharing, and in *that* way to connect with God. So with spirituality. Formerly this word meant having to do with our "spiritual"

12

life or life of private prayer with God. The basic premise underlying this concept was that the way we grow holier is by our personal prayer life primarily. And so, for instance, "spiritual books" dealt with the topic of prayer and "spiritual things" meant a set of values and realities outside the ordinary realism of human experience.

Today, however, we have broadened our grasp of what it means to grow in holiness. There are probably two big reasons for this which we will discuss later: our awareness of human psychology and the return of Catholics to the New Testament as a source of understanding of what it means to be "holy." Today we recognize that there isn't any distinction between "spiritual" growth and human growth. They are the same reality. I grow closer to God (who is Love), which is holiness, and I grow as a loving and caring person. Prayer is important because it puts me in direct contact with God, the source of my growth, but it is just one of the ways in which I grow. I also grow through self-discovery and interaction with others (for example, on a retreat). I grow through the experience of difficulty and pain and loss. I grow through my struggle to be the person I am meant to be. And it is this total reality of the growth experience which today we label "holiness" or "spirituality."

To Do:

Make a list tonight of all the opportunities you have had in the past two days to grow. Reflect upon the choices you made to grow or not to grow in the various situations.

Good News for Today:

"Bear hardships for the sake of the gospel, relying on the power of God who has saved us and called us to be holy." (2 Timothy 1:9)

Stages of the Spiritual Life

Week 2 ◇ Monday

In the late Middle Ages there were books written by St. Teresa of Avila and St. John of the Cross, two famous "spiritual writers" in Spain. At that time the word for growth was "stages in the spiritual life." It's worth discussing briefly because it is a part of our heritage and also because it has something to say to us today. The first stage is called the "purgative" stage. You're familiar with the term "purge" which means to cleanse or wipe out. The purgative stage in prayer is a time to begin to grow by getting rid of illusions, especially illusions about yourself. One of the most problematic false ideas for all of us, but especially for younger people, is a low self-esteem. If we are to learn to love God and to love others, then we need to learn first that *as ourselves* we are loved. We are lovable. Jesus may be the only person who was ever convinced that he was totally lovable. The rest of us spend a lifetime trying to arrive at that conviction. Getting rid of low self-esteem is purgation.

Also, the masks we wear, the false fronts we put up, need to be taken off. This too is part of the purgation process, the first big step in the "spiritual life." Hopefully your retreat was for you a period of purgation, a time of getting rid of warped notions of who we really are before God and others.

To Do:

Reflect on what aspect of your personality needs some "purging" or changing. Think of one way today or tomorrow you can *do* something toward that end.

14

Good News for Today:

"Now you must repent and turn to God so that your sins may be wiped out." (Acts 3:20)

The Illuminative Stage

Week 2 ◇ Tuesday

The second stage of the "spiritual life" according to St. Teresa and St. John is the "illuminative" stage. It means that if we persevere in the attempt to grow we eventually reach a point of awareness or "illumination" where we see ourselves (and others) as we truly are. For example, we recognize the distinction between our inner self and our false selves very clearly. We see that we need not be dominated by the opinions of our peers, our parents, our culture, our nation. We begin to see that we are separate and distinct people free to choose our own identity.

Sometimes after a retreat we have a brief period of real illumination. We never pass totally from one stage to another. We are always in need of "purging" or change. And we move in and out of moments of keen awareness. However, as we get older, if we are serious about growth, we arrive at greater and greater illumination. That's why most people don't wish they were younger again, or why you hear older people say: "If I knew then what I know now ..." And so to conclude this reflection let's just say that people who struggle to change and become themselves will imperceptibly grow and arrive at constantly increased levels of awareness.

To Do:

Literally, actually, take a long look at yourself in your bedroom mirror and focus on your true self, as you really are.

Good News for Today:

"Now we are seeing a dim reflection in a mirror; but then we shall be seeing face to face. The knowledge that I have now is imperfect; but then I shall know as fully as I am known." (1 Corinthians 13:12)

═══════════════════ **The Unitive Stage**

Week 2 ◇ Wednesday

The third stage of sanctity is called the "unitive" stage, coming from the Latin word for "one." A person in this stage often *feels* (not thinks) very united to God, to others, to himself or herself. It is the experience of being "at one" with ourselves and the universe. Maybe contemporary terminology for the experience of unity is feeling "together."

This stage, while it is a gift or a flash of insight and feeling, is also the result of our own hard work of cleansing ourselves of illusions. These illusions involve primarily our self-image and also our judgment about the truest values in life. This process of seeing things as they *really* are is the work of a lifetime, and that's why many people do not arrive at the unitive stage as a consistent experience until later in life.

It is not possible for you to manufacture these experiences of feeling "together" or feeling "at one." They are basically a gift of the Spirit that cannot be produced by human effort. When you have an experience of oneness be simply grateful

for it and appreciative of it. Know that your own connectedness to God and to the universe is being reaffirmed. You are being given a small preview of the kingdom of heaven.

To Do:

Go to your window (or, if possible, go to your favorite "spot" in nature) and look out at the world before you. Drink in all the beauty of life.

Good News for Today:

"All of you are one in Christ Jesus." (Galatians 3:28)

════════ Spirituality Is a Process

Week 2 ◇ Thursday

Let's look at the summation of the meaning of growth "spiritually" as we have explored over the past three days. The first stage is basically breaking through early ideas of ourselves that we grow up with (e.g., "I am unattractive, I am clumsy, I am what others think of me"). A retreat can be a significant experience in breaking through this first stage. This occurs when the way we see ourselves undergoes a shift.

The second stage, the illuminative, is when these newer, positive concepts of the self sink in and really take root. It is marked by a behavior change which takes place very gradually in the way we relate to ourselves, others and the world.

The third stage is when we can go beyond ourselves and beyond the support we get from others. It is being able to spend time alone and still feel great about ourselves without the affirmation of others. It is when we can go out of ourselves and care about others without much thought about the cost to us personally. It is a close and solid companionship with God that can constantly deepen and grow stronger.

The important thing here is not so much to try to pinpoint which stage we think we are in. Who knows anyway? What is important to ask ourselves is whether or not we are daily desirous of growing and whether we are taking concrete steps in our daily lives in order to grow.

To Do:

In writing, trace your "spiritual journey" as you see it since your childhood. Note significant events indicating personal growth. If you keep a daily journal of your reflections you may wish to record it there. If you don't keep a journal this may be a good opportunity to begin.

Good News for Today:

"If we live by the truth and in love, we shall grow in all ways into Christ." (Ephesians 4:15)

=============================== **Saints for Today**

Week 2 ◇ Friday

At one time in history people were very familiar with the stories of spiritual heroes called "the saints." One of the contributing factors in American society for the phenomenon has been the disillusionment caused by disclosure of dishonesty in the lives of so many public officials. We are slower to trust what on the outside looks like a virtuous life. In fact two of the main American heroes in the past two years have been non-humans: Yoda, the spiritual guru of "The Empire Strikes Back," and "E. T." These two figures have definitely touched the souls of the American public and yet neither of them is a human being. Maybe it's safer to trust non-humans in that they won't disappoint us.

Another problem is the definition of sainthood. What it meant to be "spiritual" even a hundred years ago is so different from the understanding of growth we have already explored. At one time sainthood implied an extraordinary life of great self-discipline and dedication to prayer. It also implied an unselfish line; perhaps that's the part we can relate to today. Perhaps that's why Mother Teresa of Calcutta is called a living saint—because of her unselfishness. People who are saints in our contemporary understanding are not people who have strange miraculous powers or who live rigid and rugged lives. Rather saints are people who are sincerely trying to grow—in love of self, love of others and love of God. Their sanctity comes not from their arrival of holiness but rather the consistency of their daily struggle. There are saints all around us.

To Do:

Think of someone whom you consider to be a "together" or holy person. Reflect upon how he or she has probably had to grow. If this is someone you know, you might even want to ask him or her about his or her struggles.

Good News for Today:

"So you are no longer aliens or foreign visitors; you are citizens like all the saints and part of God's household." (Ephesians 2:19)

Week 2 ◇ Saturday

The more we learn about what makes humans "tick" the more we are realizing what a tremendous help we can be to each other. Technology is quickly absorbing so many tasks that we no longer have to rely on other people for our *physical* needs as we once did, even twenty-five years ago. But just the opposite is true regarding our deeper, more personal needs. We see clearly now how much we need the support, the attention, the confrontation of other people to help us to grow. It is only by telling our "story" to another person that we can truly accept ourselves and become the person we are capable of becoming.

There is a term today being used more often: "spiritual director." A spiritual director is a person who helps another person to grow. Spiritual directors are not strictly counselors, although sometimes they function as such by listening to personal problems. They are chosen not because of academic degrees but because of their personal holiness and growth. A good spiritual director for a teenager is one you look up to, in whom you feel you can confide your struggles. It is an adult whose lifestyle and capacity to love you admire. The way spiritual direction works is that you approach someone and ask him or her to be your spiritual director. Now some people may not understand what that is or else may feel unworthy, and so you must explain to them what it is you are looking for. And then after that has been arranged you go to your spiritual director as often as you feel it would be helpful—no more than once a week and no less than once a month. When you visit him or her you simply talk about yourself and the struggles you are having with your own growth and in your life of prayer.

If you have chosen your spiritual director well, he or she will be able to teach you helpful ways in which to pray as well as offer suggestions for your personal growth. Over a period of time spiritual direction will prove to be a very enriching experience. It is one excellent way to keep alive the beginnings of spiritual growth experienced on a retreat. Looking upon the retreat as the sowing of seed in the soil, a spiritual director can be considered the gardener who tends the young plant until it is strong enough to survive on its own.

To Do:

Think about the possibility of establishing a relationship with a spiritual director. Consider whom you might ask. Pray about this person and see if you feel reinforced in your decision.

Good News for Today:

"As for the part in the rich soil, this is people with a noble and generous heart who have heard the word and take it to themselves and yield a harvest through their perseverance." (Luke 8:15)

Where Is God?

Week 3 ◇ Sunday

One of the advantages (and disadvantages) of our society today is that we have become very accustomed to instancy. We have instant coffee, Polaroid cameras, instant "on" built into our TV sets. Computers are sweeping across the culture rendering anything we require at the push of a button. It is truly an amazing point in history. While there are many benefits to this as technology increases its service to humanity we need to focus on one problem it aggravates: a lack of patience. We so rely on science and technology for our daily needs in an expedient way that we become quickly frustrated when technology breaks down or is unavailable. Also there is a danger that we will transfer this phenomenon into the human sphere so that, for instance, we might expect instant relationships or intimacy when that particular human reality cannot be hurried along. So too, as we turn this week to the topic of prayer, we need to realize that a relationship with God is really something that we need to build and that has to grow over time. There is no magic prayer formula we can say that will instantly produce a deep bond between us and the Lord. And yet on the other hand it's healthy to be impatient for closeness to him. In the New Testament Jesus tells us that the "Kingdom of God is at hand" which is simply saying that the Lord is among us *right* now. And so we do have immediate access to him. But for the bond between us to so develop that it remains unshaken during difficult times takes lots of communication (called prayer) over the months and years of our lives. Just as it takes time for a human friendship to grow, so is this true with our relationship with Jesus.

To Do:

Search out the song recorded by George Harrison, "My Sweet Lord," and listen to it as a prayer of impatience by today's civilization for closeness with the Lord.

Good News for Today:

" 'The time has come,' he said, 'and the Kingdom of God is close at hand. Repent and believe the good news.' " (Mark 1:15)

Seek and you will find.
Ask and you will be answered.
Knock and the door will open.

So I sought and found,
   I asked and was answered,
   I knocked and the door opened.

My finding was a deeper search.
My answer was a profounder question.
My door opened into a more fascinating door.

My deeper search enlarged my heart.
My profounder question stretched my mind.
My more fascinating door quickened my spirit.

I've become a pilgrim delighting in my venture.
I've become a trailblazer excited by my expedition.
I've become a pioneer stimulated by my trek.

Jesus said to me: "Come, follow me."
My answer: "I'm coming—I'm becoming—I'm overcome."

                                     Amen

Who Is Your God?

Week 3 ◊ Monday

As we get older our understanding of who God is often shifts. As a little child perhaps there was a picture or statue of Jesus in your bedroom from which you derived an image of who he is. Or it could have been in a book or a film or in your parish church that you were given a picture of who God or Jesus Christ is. Just as you are maturing in so many other ways as you grow into young adulthood, so too it's necessary to grow up in our image of God. Unfortunately many people retain their childhood understanding of him their entire lives. But just the fact that you went on a retreat and are following these meditations means that you are serious about maturing in the Lord.

There is an interesting little book by J. B. Phillips entitled *Your God Is Too Small.* In it he discusses several "inadequate" concepts that people have of God. These concepts include a "Grand Old Man," a "Resident Policemen," and a sentimental "Pale Galilean." It's probably a good time for you to think about your image of God or Jesus. Our visual picture of him says a lot about our ideas of who he is and how he relates to us. Often when we are young, we have ideas of God as a sort of security blanket as well as a performer of wonders and miracles. The image of him as a close friend with whom we can be in intimate relationships is a concept that develops as we get older. In fact, just as we can grow to know a close friend in ever new ways over an entire lifetime, so also can we grow in our concept of God.

To Do:

If you have a spiritual director, talk to him or her about your concept of the Lord. Or you can discuss it with a parent or a friend, or reflect on it yourself. How long has it been since your idea of who he is has changed at all?

Good News for Today:

" 'But you,' he said, 'who do *you* say I am?' " (Luke 9:20)

Dear Friend:

I wanted to send this short note to say how much I love you and care about you. I saw you yesterday as you were talking with your friends. I waited all day hoping you would want to talk to me. As the day faded, I gave you a sunset to close your

25

day and a cool breeze to rest you, and I waited but you never came. Obviously it hurts me, but I still love you because I am your friend.

I saw you as you started to fall asleep and I really wanted to touch your head, so I spilled moonlight on your pillow and your face. Again I waited, wanting to rush down so we could talk. I have so many gifts for you. You got up late and rushed off. My tears were in the rain.

Some days you look so sad—so all alone. It makes my heart ache because I understand. My friends let me down and hurt me many times but I love you.

If you would only listen to me: I love you. I try to tell you this in the blue sky and in the quiet green grass. I whisper it in the leaves and breathe it in the color of flowers. I shout it to you in the mountain streams and give the birds love songs to sing. I clothe you with warm sunshine and perfume the air with nature's scents. My love for you is deeper than the ocean and bigger than the biggest want or need in your head. If only you knew how much I want to walk and talk with you.

I know how tough it is. I really know—and I want to help. I would like you to meet my Father. He wants to help you too. My Father is that way.

Just call me—ask me—talk with me. Please don't forget me. I have so much to share with you. All right, I won't bother you any further—for now. You are free to choose me. It is your decision. I have chosen you, and because of this I will wait—and wait—and wait—because I love you.

Your friend,

Jesus

by Patti, age 16

I WONDER IF GOD HAS A FACE. DO YOU THINK HE EVER SLEEPS? DO YOU THINK HE TAKES DAYS OFF? WILL WE BE ABLE TO FLY IN HEAVEN? ARE THERE CLOUDS IN HEAVEN? ARE ANIMALS ALLOWED IN HEAVEN? ARE THESE QUESTIONS TOO HARD?

Where Is Your God?

Week 3 ◊ Tuesday

In the past when we have discussed the whereabouts of God we have often pointed up and away to heaven. In more recent years we have been focusing on the nearness of God to us and the possibility of a relationship with him. Thus we have also focused on the presence of his Spirit in our midst. In St. John's Gospel it says that in Jesus God "dwelt" among us. The actual translation of the Greek word for "dwelt" is "pitched a tent." This is pretty strong language St. John chose to tell us how close God came to us in his Son. It's the ascension story where Jesus goes up into heaven from a mountaintop that makes us think of him as removed or far away. But what that story indicates is simply that Jesus is not *physically* among us anymore. The other side is that he is very much with us today in his Spirit.

Another place that God's Spirit "dwells" is right within us. He is the source of our life itself, and his presence was intensified at our baptism and even more at our confirmation (which perhaps you are still in preparation for). This is a great way to think of Jesus Christ—as always present within us at the very core of our being. What a help this realization is in dealing with our human loneliness at any time.

While it is true that heaven or the after-life exists in a realm unknown to us and that God is truly present there, it is more helpful in our daily lives to realize his presence close to us—in the world, in other people, in ourselves.

To Do:

Take a few minutes in a quiet place to focus on the presence of Jesus within your heart and soul. Try to pray to his Spirit within.

Good News for Today:

"Your body, you know, is the temple of the Holy Spirit who is in you since you received him from God." (1 Corinthians 19:13)

How Do You Pray?
Week 3 ◇ Wednesday

Let's examine a few ways to pray for the rest of this week. Probably as a kid you knew of two ways to pray: asking God for things and thanking God for the things. And that's fine for little kids. But as we mature in our understanding of who the Lord is and where he is, we also need to mature in the way that we relate to him which is called prayer. Prayer is simply our communication with God. And just as you no longer see your parents as the dispensers of rewards and punishments but as people to relate to in love and friendship, so too you are hopefully growing out of the "gimme God" syndrome.

Jesus certainly taught us to ask for good things from the Father. He also has assured us of God's attention when we make requests. But that our prayers will be answered to our particular specifications is not guaranteed. That would presuppose a God capable of being manipulated by human wishes. God is our friend, and as such he wants to be with us in our struggles and to give us his Spirit to get us through every difficulty. Our welfare is his concern; he cares for us personally and individually. But to turn him into a sort of spiritual Santa Claus who doles out presents from his magic bag is to really cheapen our relationship with him. Do you do that to any of your other friends—make them constantly give you things? Of course not. We have been created as intelligent creatures with both the responsibility and the freedom to work out our own solutions to life's many challenges. This freedom is the root of our creaturehood. To rob us of it would be to rob us of our humanness. Also, God is concerned that we know he is there for us, that he will be with us in our struggle and that in *his own way* he will answer our prayer for his help. And so this type of maturing in our understanding of asking God for things is extremely important if we are to grow out of our spiritual childhood.

To Do:

Reflect briefly upon your own maturity or immaturity in this area of prayer. Ask yourself if you are really willing to let go of childish ways so that you might grow into spiritual adulthood.

Good News for Today:

"If you then, who are evil, know how to give your children what is good, how much more will the heavenly Father give the Holy Spirit to those who ask him!" (Luke 11:13)

Week 3 ◇ Thursday

One of the best and simplest ways to pray is called meditation. This means thinking about things in a reflective type of way. Usually it is best to use a book as an aid. For example, if you are using this book right now in a reflective way (as opposed to just reading it straight through), then you are meditating. The way to "pray" this book or any religious book is to read a line, a paragraph or a page and then put the book down and think about what the material you just read means or how it has an application in your own life. If you start to daydream in this process it helps to have the book to return to so that you can read a little more. A good time frame for a young person to meditate is anywhere from ten to twenty minutes per day. A quiet place without distraction is important, as is being in a comfortable position, but not too comfortable. Don't lie down to meditate because it's too easy to daydream or doze.

The best book in the world for meditation used each day by Christians all over the world is the Gospel contained in the New Testament. There are four versions of the Gospel written by Matthew, Mark, Luke, and John. Some stories are the same in the Gospel versions and some are different. Later in this book we are going to spend several days just showing different ways of meditating on the Gospel. So, in conclusion, let's say that meditation is a form of prayer, very helpful to many in keeping God's word alive and meaningful in their daily lives.

To Do:

If you have chosen a spiritual director in either a formal or an informal sense, discuss a daily plan with him or her for a two week period which could help you to develop a habit of meditative prayer.

Good News for Today:

"Think hard about all this, and put it into practice, and everyone will be able to see how you are advancing." (1 Timothy 4:15)

Alone with God (Contemplation)

Week 3 ◇ Friday

There is another form of prayer different from meditation. It is called "contemplation." This excellent form of prayer is seldom experienced in our society. The reason we say that is because first of all it requires that we be totally relaxed and slowed down with all our interior motors "off." Our society is so geared to activity and achievement that it is very hard for most of us to just stop and be still. The most important thing to turn off in contemplation prayer is the activity of the mind: memory, imagination, the thought process. It is quite different from meditation which relies on the mind's activity. Contemplation suspends the mind's activity. It is a simple attempt, as it says in the Bible, to "be still and know that I am God." It is the deepest form of communication with God because it is the experience of love itself. On a human level meditation resembles two friends' communication with each other, while contemplation resembles two people who know each other so well that they can just gaze upon each other without words and feel an intense love.

Contemplative experiences cannot be forced. Sometimes they just happen, as for example, when we are overcome on a beach by the roaring of the sea or the beauty of a sunset. This is called a "natural" contemplative experience. The effect of nature is so profound that we suspend all our thought process if only for a few moments. This can also happen in prayer sometimes—we can be so overwhelmed by an experience of God's love that we just bask in that feeling for a few moments without having any thoughts. Generally this deeper form of prayer is a gift given to those who have been faithful for some time to daily meditation.

To Do:

Try using a watch with a minute hand, to see if you can sit still for just two minutes with your mind a complete blank. When thoughts creep up on you just gently let them go to float off into space.

Good News for Today:

"If anyone loves me he will keep my word, and my Father will love him, and we shall come to him and make our home with him." (John 14:23)

I have found it
I have seen it
I have been it
I was taken by it, and it and I were we
I was doubtful at first that it wanted me
I was amazed that it did
I was overtaken by its strength
I experienced a fullness that was unexperienceable
I realized that it has always been there
I know that it always will be

Peter, age 17

This reflection, written by a teenager, is his retelling of what a contemplation experience is like.

YOU GET HIGH ON GOD?
DO YOU SMOKE HIM
OR DO YOU DRINK HIM?

Asceticism and Prayer

Week 3 ◊ Saturday

Asceticism is a harsh sounding word. It comes from a Greek word meaning "to exercise." It refers not to prayer itself but to our preparation for prayer, serious prayer. We are talking about atmosphere, first of all. Asceticism implies that we have the self-control to shut our door and remove ourselves for a short time at least from the noisy confusion of the world. It means we have the self-discipline to turn off the radio and perhaps to take the phone off the hook for fifteen minutes so that we will not be disturbed. Asceticism means that we choose to sit upright while we pray rather than lie stretched out on a couch in order that we might be fully attentive to our communication with the Lord. Asceticism also means that we discipline ourselves (gently) to pray for the amount of time we have promised for ourselves, no matter how many distractions come our way.

In a more remote sense diet and physical exercise are ascetical practices related to prayer. It's really hard to focus on our communication on a purely "spiritual" level in the narrow sense of that word if we have a full stomach or are feeling the effects of caffeine or alcohol or some other substance. Prayer time needs to be removed from normal time and party time. The more balanced and nutritious our diet, the better "tone" our bodies will have and the more we will feel prepared to turn to prayer. So too with exercise. Exercise tones our bodies and clears our minds so that we are able more easily to turn to God in prayer. In fact, the best time to pray is often after a good physical workout, transforming the natural "high" of that activity to an opportunity to commune with the Spirit.

35

To Do:

Examine your diet and physical exercise in light of this discussion. Is there some resolution you can make for the next two weeks?

Good News for Today:

"Then Jesus was led by the Spirit out into the wilderness to be tempted by the devil. He fasted for forty days and forty nights, after which he was very hungry." (Matthew 4:1–2)

Relating to Myself

Week 4 ◊ Sunday

Believe it or not, one of the toughest people to relate to is myself. Why? Because we don't truly love ourselves enough. Psychologists tell us that a lack of self-love is at the root of most of our problems in relating to others. According to a survey of Merton Strommen entitled *The Five Crises of Youth* low self-esteem was ranked by teenagers as their biggest problem (seven thousand youths were interviewed, ages fifteen to seventeen, in various religious denominations). Studies also indicated that there is a close correlation between teenagers who have a low self-image, and teenagers who feel that God won't bother to answer their prayers.

Why do we have a low self-image (and we all do to some extent)? Well nobody is quite sure. Some people today are saying that this psychological "woundedness" that we carry is the effect of original sin or the human condition. These people would also say that Jesus is the only man who ever lived who had a perfect self-image—that he is the only person who has ever been able to totally accept the fact that he was totally loved by God. And the rest of us spend an entire lifetime growing in the acceptance of this truth that God loves us unconditionally. Of course we all know that in our intellect, but we mean *feeling* a hundred percent acceptable to God and therefore to ourselves and everybody else.

Low self-esteem has many forms. Some people who have it withdraw from others and from the challenge of relating. Others spend their entire day trying to avoid humiliation, feeling that they are under the scrutiny and the judgment of the human race. Still others brag and boast and put other people down; they need to do this because they feel so very terrible about who they are. It is low self-esteem that also makes us jealous and devious and even cruel in our relationships. Whatever form it takes, a poor self-concept is a very spiritually debilitating reality. Hopefully your recent retreat gave you a boost in good feelings about yourself and how you are loved. Intimate and honest friendships are very crucial to the development of self-esteem. We need the experience of being loved and accepted just as we are by at least one friend. It is often helpful to talk with a counselor or teacher or some respected older person about poor self-esteem. Such conversations over time often radically alter how we see ourselves.

To Do:

On a scale of one to ten, rank your self-image. If it is five or below, try to talk to someone about how you feel about yourself.

Good News for Today:

"We are to love, then, because he first loved us." (1 John 4:19)

Relating to Friends

Week 4 ◊ Monday

There is so much written today about the significance of human friendship. And while it is one of the most powerful and life-giving experiences we can have, it is also one of the most difficult. Greeting cards in drug stores could make you think that friendship is all sweetness and light, sunsets and flowers. No so. The development of a friendship is a very challenging road. If the challenge is taken seriously, then there indeed are beautiful moments to be had. Let's focus on the nature of this challenge.

First of all, a friend is someone to whom I choose to reveal myself. The medieval monks used the term "soul friend"—as someone to whom I reveal my very soul, my very self. This revelation is a process which grows as trust grows. It is a very important risk that everyone should take in life—to be totally known (i.e., as much as we can be) by one other human being who accepts us exactly as we truly are. It is this acceptance which in turn enables us to accept ourselves better, as we discussed yesterday. And as beautiful as this experience of acceptance is in regard to ourselves, so is it in regard to another.

Secondly, a friend is someone with whom I am honest about not only who I am but who he or she is. Now this honesty can be difficult to express. Many of us have a hard time telling our friends how much we value them, how we rely on them, and how we truly love them. And yet the expression of these feelings is crucial to the deepening of the friendship. It should never be presumed that our friends know how we feel if we have never told them. It's again a risk because we open ourselves to a possible rejection just as we do in other aspects of self-revelation. And yet it's worth the risk involved.

Negative feelings about aspects of your friends' behavior also need to be expressed. Many people can reveal themselves and tell their friends how much they love them, etc., but can never bring themselves to be really honest about any negative feelings they may also have toward those persons. If this step does not occur, a friendship will never come to full maturity. Two people who are close need to know that their relationship is strong enough and safe enough to also express anger, resentment, jealousy, and any other negative feelings. Once this dimension has been built into a friendship, then the relationship is truly strengthened into a bond that can last for a long, long time.

To Do:

Think about one friend to whom you need to express either positive or negative feelings. Try to do that tomorrow, even if only in some small way.

Good News for Today:

"For I am certain of this: neither death nor life, no angel, no prince, nothing that exists, nothing still to come, not any power, or height or depth, nor any created thing, can ever come between us." (Romans 8:30–39)
(This model for our relationship with Christ can also be the model for a deep human friendship achieved through risk and honesty.)

I Need Your Help

I want to ask you for a favor,
A big favor; it means very much to me.
I need your help to do something.

I'm trying to get to know you.
I want to be your friend.

But this is very difficult.
It is not at all easy.
Not because you are particularly hard to know.
But I am particularly poor at discovering you.

You see it is one thing to want to do something,
And another to make the effort to do it,
And still another to actually do it.

In other words, sometimes it may not seem
    like I want to be your friend.
And maybe I don't know just how to do it,
But don't let that fool you.
I'm nevertheless trying.

That's where you come in.
I'm kind of new at this,
And naturally clumsy at first,
So you've got to let me try.
You have to give me a chance.
That's why I need your help.

More important than that, though,
It's a two-way street,
Implying an effort from both of us.
It's a joint venture.
That is why I need your help.

I want to know you.
That's why I need your help.

Anonymous

From *Friendship,* St. Mary's College Press, 1976, p. 26

Relating to Parents

Week 4 ◊ Tuesday

The hardest thing about children relating to parents is that children view parents as parents and parents view children as children. In other words they see each other in roles as opposed to persons with needs, desires, strengths and weaknesses. Late teenage years are usually the time of a budding awareness that one's parents are indeed people with feelings of their own.

A very difficult ordeal for most parents is the departure of their children from the "nest" of the home. Of course, good parents raise their children to be independent and intellectually know that it is good for their offspring to strike out into the world. However the emotions or the feeling level is often quite in another place because it is so very hard for people to "let go" of someone they have nurtured and cherished for so long. This problem is compounded by the fact that late adolescence is a time when children begin to be independent while still living at home—for example, by always being "on the go" and out of the home. This type of behavior can often be interpreted by parents (who are usually emotionally vulnerable at this time) as an unloving attitude toward the family, and it can cause them as parents to feel that they are being discarded by their son or daughter. During this period a great deal of sensitivity toward where each other is in the life process can help alleviate a lot of pain. Also, very frank communication helps tremendously—not about what one *thinks* of the other's behavior but rather how the other's behavior makes one *feel.*

To Do:

Reflect upon your relationship with your parents. Try to find one small way tomorrow that will demonstrate to them how much you really do care about them.

Good News for Today:

"A man (or woman) can have no greater love than to lay down his (or her) life for his (or her) friends (includes parents)." (John 15:13)

=== **Parents**

Week 4 ◊ Wednesday

Today's reflection is written by Doug, age 19.

I think the biggest element of establishing a good relationship with a parent is realizing that parents are people too—people whom God created. Too many times we take our parents for granted. We find ourselves saying: "My mom was in a lousy mood," yet not realizing that she has a right to be irritable once in a while. We don't appreciate that she may have had a bad day. A parent has feelings too. Just as teenagers bring home tribulations from school, so too a parent may come home from work with something upsetting. The key here for a teenager to see is that this is the time to show your love to your parents. When you see them hurting, just care a little bit. A parent usually can realize how difficult it can be for you to take such a big step.

The saying, "Nobody's perfect," also applies a great deal to our parents. Kids tend to feel that a parent's mistake is unforgivable. As teenagers, we generally make many mistakes. Yet when hurt by our parents, we sometimes become more irritated and tough than they do.

The fourth Commandment says to honor thy father and mother. This Commandment, when thought about carefully, is perhaps one of the easiest for a teenager to keep. It takes the reaching of a maturity level. Once a teenager is able to realize that his parents have feelings too, he is capable of living in a "two way street" relationship. Parents are crying out to be loved and understood just as much as teenagers. When a teenager looks at a parent as a person and not someone created to "serve" him, he then and only then is honoring them. It's hard to keep in mind that God created parents with just as many faults as kids. God realizes that parents are human beings, and human beings make mistakes and have weaknesses. Teenagers must strive to become aware of this fact as well.

Why is it always the job of the parent to begin communication? Too many parent–child relationships lack this key element. I feel that teenagers need to wake up and take some responsibility to be open and honest with their parents. One thing parents are entitled to is honesty from their teenager. There can be no successful means of communication without it. How many times do we deceive our parents? We should trust our parents to be fair about things. Too many times we lie or hide things from them because we are afraid of the word "no." We feel the need to lie about where we go on Friday night. An example of this is when we say we are going to the movies with a friend but end up at a keg party. We have to stop and ask ourselves: Is this keg party worth the risk of shattering the trust my parents have in me? For once parents feel that they can no longer trust their teenager, it is extremely difficult for a teenager to re-establish it.

No one is saying that communication in this way is easy. We must believe that it is God's will that we give it our best shot.

To Do:

Let one of your parents know how much you love him or her either verbally or in a note tomorrow.

44

Good News for Today:

"My children, our love is not to be just words or mere talk, but something real and active." (John 3:18)

═══════════ Relating to the Earth

Week 4 ◊ Thursday

One of the awarenesses we are growing in today is how intimately we are connected with the earth and our physical environment. Man's role is seen today not as a subduer of the earth but rather as relating to the ecology and respecting it for his own personal benefit. The air we breathe, the water we drink and the ground we walk on all have a connection to us.

Very often in this age of high technology those of us who live outside of rural areas lose sight of our connectedness with all of nature. For us therefore it becomes very important to "return" to nature by going to the seashore or the lakeside or by taking a walk in the woods. In some way at some level deep within us we can feel at home in such surroundings, as if we had been away for a while and have returned to where we belong.

To Do:

Take some time out of your day today or tomorrow and physically take yourself to a place in nature where you can be cut off from other people and the noise of the world.

Good News for Today:

Today instead of a reading from the New Testament ponder these words of Henry Thoreau from his book *Walden:* "I went to the woods because I wished to live deliberately, to confront only the essential facts of life, and see if I could not learn what it had to teach, and not, when I came to die, discover that I had not lived. I did not wish to live what was not life, living is so dear; nor did I wish to practice resignation, unless it was quite necessary. I wanted to live deep and suck out all the marrow of life."

===== **Relating to Older People**

Week 4 ◇ Friday

One of the most unfortunate developments in North American society is the categorization of people by chronological age. A youth culture has emerged with the reinforcement of the advertising world. While teenagers and young adults need their peers very much for support and relationships, they also need to connect with middle-aged and older adults. This is necessary for several reasons.

First of all, there is an unreality if we relate only to our age group. It puts us out of touch with a part of ourselves to do so. For younger people, it puts them out of touch with the part of themselves that is growing older and separating from childhood. Sometimes it's scary at a deep level within to think of our own aging process, and somehow we think we can avoid that aspect of ourselves by avoiding contact with older age groups. But by so doing we are running from truth and not experiencing the freedom we could have by letting go of the fear of aging.

Another reason we need contact with older people is because they can help us understand our own lives more clearly, since they have already been through experiences we are now having. Their insight and advice can save us a lot of hardship and needless worry.

Just one more reason to consider is that the whole point of living is to grow in love and in freedom. Ideally, as we advance in years we should also advance in freedom, letting go of fears, of caring so much about what others think of us and of knowing what the *true* values in life are. Now it is certainly true that some adults get stuck in the web of searching for security and becoming rigid, extremely conservative and closed minded. And this is surely not desirable. But those adults who do grasp the true meaning of life and become freer and more open and loving as they get older are wonderfully exciting people and well worth knowing. Their own zest for life is contagious and so helpful for younger people in the process of dealing with the beginnings of adulthood. The folk singer/ writer Bob Dylan had a line that refers to this growth in inner freedom: "I was older then ... I am younger than that now."

To Do:

Think of an older person you admire and plan to have a conversation with him or her about his or her ideas of the aging process.

Good News for Today:

"Then he said, 'I tell you solemnly, unless you change and become like little children you will never enter the Kingdom of heaven.' " (Matthew 18:3)

Relating to the World

Week 4 ◇ Saturday

The term "global village" is a very popular one today. It refers to the fact that the world has become smaller due to transportation, communications, and economic interdependence. We can no longer think of our country in isolation from the rest of the world. Survival depends on our network of relationships with everybody.

All of this is very complex. But issues of justice and peace come into play here. Sometimes affluent countries take advantage of poorer peoples in poorer countries to produce or raise goods more cheaply. Sometimes rich people make a profit from the hardship of poor people. This is a rather simplistic statement, and there are lots of ramifications, especially political ones, to economic situations. The main thing here for the Christian is simply to realize that the world is a community and that peoples and nations are interdependent on one another. This awareness in itself is very important. After that it's a question of reading newspapers and pertinent literature which can inform a person about existing injustices on an international scale.

To Do:

Read the newspaper today or watch the news on TV.

Good News for Today:

"May they all be one, Father; may they be one in us." (John 17:21)

Sacraments-Baptism

Week 5 ◊ Sunday

The main trouble with the sacraments is that by labeling them we tend to think of them as "things." In reality the word "sacrament" refers to the specialness of the "meeting" between Jesus Christ and the person. There are many ways we can be united to Jesus, of course: by reading his Gospel, spending time in prayer, helping the poor and needy, and so on. However it has always been believed by the Christian community that there is a special encounter between God and persons at significant moments of the human life cycle. Some of these encounters were spoken about by Jesus himself; some were not. It is now the consensus of our community (the Roman Catholic Church) that there are seven of these special moments.

The first of these special encounters is called "baptism," coming from a Greek word meaning "to immerse." This refers to the first, initial meeting with God we experience as babies. That's why it's called a "sacrament of initiation." In early Christian times the experience of converting to belief in Jesus Christ was symbolized by being immersed in water. People would totally go under water and then come up symbolically into a new life. They would receive a new name and a new white robe to further symbolize this inner change to becoming a believer. Today a person's family in a sense ushers him or her into the faith as an infant. Instead of total immersion we pour water over the baby's head.

At the moment of baptism we say that we receive grace (which means God's strength) to live the Christian life. We also say that the effects of original sin are removed from the person. Maybe as a little child you once thought of these effects of original sin as a sort of blemish on the person's "soul" or spiritual life. There are many theories on exactly what these effects are. A simple explanation is that these effects equal the human condition with all its flaws and vulnerabilities, physical and emotional, and all its limitations. The grace of baptism assures us that one day, in our dying and rising, the pain and limits of this human condition will be overcome.

Also, our baptism is our entrance into God's family, the Christian community. It is our own initiation rite joining us to God as our Father and also connecting us with all our brothers and sisters in the Church. Your retreat was a very intense experience of the possibilities of this baptismal community.

To Do:

Ask your parents if they have a copy of your baptismal certificate. Read it over and meditate on your membership in the Christian community.

Good News for Today:

"All baptized in Christ, you have all clothed yourselves in Christ, and there are no more distinctions between Jew and Greek, slave and free, male and female, but all of you are one in Christ Jesus." (Galatians 3:27–28)

Confirmation

Week 5 ◊ Monday

A second sacrament of initiation is confirmation which most people in the United States receive as teenagers. It's more or less the completion of baptism in that it gives us a chance to

SO YOU'RE INTO GOD
NOW, ARE YA?

act for ourselves (which we couldn't do as babies) in committing ourselves to Jesus Christ and his way of life. Confirmation therefore should always be entered into freely without coercion and should always reflect a personal choice. If a person has trouble making such a commitment, he or she should wait to receive that sacrament, since there is no special age at which confirmation should be received.

Again it will help to think of the sacraments as special moments with God which only make sense in the context of a relationship with him. Confirmation is not a *thing* to receive before you get out of high school. The theology (which means the understanding the Church has) of confirmation focuses on the "Holy Spirit." The Holy Spirit has been symbolized by a dove very often in the Church. But it does not mean that the Holy Spirit is a bird or something like that. The Holy Spirit is simply another way of saying that Jesus' spirit is still present among us. It is another moment of grace or strength to follow a holy way of life in the adult years.

Probably confirmation is the most significant sacrament to young adults in the sense that it summarizes the whole Christian vocation. Growing up as a child we don't realize that following Jesus is a *free* choice—that he gives all of us an invitation to which we may or may not respond. Somehow as a small child we can think of the Christian vocation as a given, like our nationality, our race, our color, etc. But as we get older we begin to realize that our religion is not an automatic thing. Of course our parents have probably nurtured us in the faith, but it is still up to us in adulthood to accept or reject what we have been taught.

To Do:

Think about your own confirmation. Ask yourself if you follow Jesus and his teachings out of your own inner convictions or out of a sense of duty to the way you have been raised—or both. How do you feel about being his follower?

"I, personally, am free; I am an apostle and I have seen Jesus our Lord." (1 Corinthians 9:1)

===================================== **Eucharist**

Week 5 ◊ Tuesday

The word "Eucharist" refers to the most special and intimate union between God and humanity. It is the moment when we literally consume the very person of Jesus Christ under the forms of bread and wine. It's the sacrament that was instituted by Jesus himself at the Last Supper when he told his apostles to eat his body and drink his blood, for by so doing they would live forever.

This sacrament is a very great mystery and beyond our understanding. There's an "old time religion" expression, "Better felt than telt," meaning better experienced than explained if you want to understand it. So it is with the Eucharist (which we usually call "Holy Communion"). By receiving it at Mass we can have a real experience of union with Jesus, and many people who go to Communion regularly can even feel his presence within them in a spiritual sense. The Eucharist is the greatest gift we could have from God, and it gives us much grace.

To "consume" a beloved one is not alien to our psychology. We talk about loving a baby so much we could "eat it up." People who are deeply in love long to be consumed by the other in a spiritual sense or to be able to break the bonds that isolate us from each other as human beings. And so the idea of consuming Jesus should not strike us as strange but rather very much in keeping with human psychology.

The Eucharist is also the source of strength we have to live a loving life because it *is* God who *is* Love. We all know how easy it is to talk about love, and we all know pretty much what it is to act in loving ways. But given our many weaknesses and the frailty of our human condition, we often fail in loving. Perhaps you made resolutions on your retreat (more than a month ago) which you find unable to keep. This is why the Eucharist is so important. It gives us the "grace" or strength that we need in order to keep loving even when it is difficult. Some people receive Holy Communion every single day to help them in their life of love. It is important to receive the Eucharist at least once a week in order to sustain the Christian life.

To Do:

Go to Mass one day within the next week (outside of Sunday) and receive Holy Communion.

Good News for Today:

"God is love, and anyone who lives in love lives in God, and God lives in him." (1 John 4:16)

Reconciliation

Week 5 ◇ Wednesday

Reconciliation is another sacrament which was instituted by Jesus at the Last Supper when he told his apostles: "Whose sins you shall forgive they are forgiven . . ." This established the apostles—or, today, the priests—as the representatives in the Christian family of Jesus himself invested with the power of removing sin in his name.

Today a lot of teenagers criticize this sacrament because they don't understand it. First of all, penance does not excuse us from asking forgiveness of the person we have offended. That is always an important part of reconciliation. "So why do you have to tell your sins to a priest?" Well, we're not totally sure why Jesus established this practice in the way he did, but we do have some hunches. Maybe it's that Jesus knew human psychology so well that he realized we still often feel guilty even after making an apology. Maybe he knew that the best thing for our security is hearing an official, appointed representative of his very self telling us that we are truly and forever forgiven.

This sacrament or special meeting with Jesus should be sought out:

(a) when we have done something seriously wrong;

(b) when there is an unfavorable pattern developing in our behavior;

(c) when we need to pause and take stock of our Christian life.

This sacrament is also important because it strengthens us with grace to live in a world which often tugs us away from goodness.

To Do:

Call a priest with whom you feel you can talk and make an appointment to receive the sacrament of penance.

Good News for Today:

"After saying this he breathed on them and said: 'Receive the Holy Spirit. For those whose sins you forgive, they are forgiven; for those whose sins you retain, they are retained.'" (John 20:23)

Week 5 ◇ Thursday

Any life choice is a sacred event in that we all have a vocation to fulfill so that we can more and more become our true selves. But the Christian community has given the distinction of sacrament to two of these choices. It has done so with matrimony because it is the way of life chosen by the majority of Christian people. This way of life involves a deep and permanent commitment of love. Being in relationship with another person is a wonderful way to grow into human maturity. We need the experiences of both acceptance and challenge to become the most we can be. And so the Christian community has always looked upon this deep commitment to another as a special moment with the Lord (or "sacrament").

Holy orders refers to ordination to the official priesthood of the Church. Priests are leaders in the community as well as in charge of preaching and presiding at the liturgy (Mass) and the celebration of the sacraments. Because ordination is such a special form of service to God and his people the Church considers holy orders to be one of the seven sacraments.

Another way of life is the single lifestyle. This option affords people a lot of freedom to be dedicated to a career or life project and also enhances their availability to others. As we are becoming increasingly psychologically aware as a culture, we are realizing that human beings are so varied that there is no one lifestyle mold into which all people should fit. Another aspect of the single life is that friendships are extremely significant for support and fulfillment.

Still another way of life is traditionally called the "religious life." Perhaps this terminology isn't the best, since all the vocations of a Christian person are religious. A better term is "the vowed life" lived in community. The vows of poverty, celibacy and obedience to superiors comprise this lifestyle as well as belonging in a very real way to a community of other similarly vowed persons. Members of this type of life (often called "brothers" or "sisters") generally live a life of service in a career like nursing or teaching or social work. Priests can also choose to be members of these vowed communities. Some communities of contemplatives (monks and nuns) live lives of intense prayer and silence. Vowed community life offers a beautiful and challenging alternative to a Christian intent on following Jesus very closely.

To Do:

Think about the many options open to you as a young Christian.

Good News for Today:

"He who is not with me is against me; and he who does not gather with me scatters." (Luke 11:23)

Anointing of the Sick

Week 5 ◊ Friday

Another time in life when we need to have a special moment with the Lord is when we are ill or near death. This sacrament is also to give grace and strength. Sometimes the grace actually heals the person physically. Sometimes it gives courage to sustain a long illness or chronic condition. Still other times it helps a person to die peacefully and trustfully. In the

Gospel we see that very many of the special encounters of Jesus were with people who were seriously ill. The community considers this special form of meeting the Lord a sacrament.

At one time this sacrament was called "last rites" because it was administered close to the hour of death. Today we have returned to an understanding of this sacrament held by the early Christian community—that it also can strengthen us for daily life in the here and now. And that is why people who are preparing for surgery or who are chronically ill are invited to receive this sacrament.

To Do:

When we become ill we know how good it makes us feel when other people take care of us and visit us. Reflect today on your own capacity to "anoint the sick" by visiting them and encouraging them. We can all be "sacraments" or extensions of Christ to each other, strengthening each other in the journey of life. Make a resolution to visit someone this week who is ill or confined to a nursing home.

Good News for Today:

"And this is what we ask you to do, brothers: warn the idlers, give courage to those who are apprehensive, care for the weak and be patient with everyone. . . . You must all think of what is best for each other and for the community." (1 Thessalonians 5:14–16)

I'VE LEARNED THAT WITH JESUS AS OUR SAVIOR WE HAVE NOTHING TO FEAR. YOU GO FIRST.

Week 5 ◇ Saturday

Yesterday we talked about encouraging the members of our community who are ill. This is one concrete way that we can be "Christ" to each other. We said on Sunday that sacraments are special meetings with Jesus and they are defined as such by the Church. But in actuality there are hundreds and thousands of opportunities for each of us to personally extend Jesus' touch in the world. If we examine the Gospel, it becomes very noticeable that Jesus went around "touching" people's lives in a variety of ways: he listened, he healed, he held, he touched, he consoled and encouraged. Each of these occasions was in its own way a "sacramental" moment, a meeting with Jesus. And so it follows that we who are extensions of Jesus can be "sacraments" to one another, not in the defined sense of the seven sacraments but in a general way. Every time we touch other persons or smile at them or encourage them or help them in some way we are living "sacramentally." After all, we are the living embodiment of Jesus Christ in the world. There is a crucifix in a church in Europe which had the arms and legs of the corpus broken off during a bombing raid. The crucifix was put up again with a sign beneath it: "You are my hands, you are my feet."

To Do:

Go out of your way to affirm or encourage someone today or tomorrow.

"There is one Lord, Jesus Christ, through whom all things come and through whom we exist." (1 Corinthians 8:6)

What Is Morality?

Week 6 ◊ Sunday

Morality is a word that is often misunderstood. Many people, especially older people, see the word as synonymous with sexual behavior—immoral referring to inappropriate or wrong sexual behavior. Still other people understand the word "moral" character to refer to honesty in business dealings. Both of these understandings of the terminology are very limited in scope. They have probably developed for cultural reasons, and perhaps new words are needed to express the broader range of right and wrong behavior.

Morality and immorality refer to inner attitudes that people have as well as to their external behavior. The idea is simply that the feeling of love within our hearts or the idea that loving is correct within our intellects is simply not enough. Love must be translated from feelings and thinking into concrete action in order to be real and credible. Loving is not only an interior disposition, it is action with and for others. It is precisely this action which is the living out of Christianity and following Jesus Christ's way of life.

Many popular songs over the last twenty years have had beautiful and meaningful lyrics about the nature of love. But if ideas about love just remain within us like lyrics in a song and never get translated into action, then the words of love are empty and meaningless. Sometimes a retreat can be compared

61

to listening to the lyrics of a love song, but the real test of the loving comes in the living that follows the retreat.

To Do:

Go out of your way for someone once in the next twenty-four hours, in a way that you did not intend before reading this meditation.

Good News for Today:

"Take the case, my brothers, of someone who has never done a single good act but claims that he has faith. Will that faith save him? If one of the brothers or sisters is in need of clothes and has not enough food to live on, and one of you says to them, 'I wish you well; keep yourself warm and eat plenty' without giving them the bare necessities of life, then what good is that? Faith is like that: if good works do not go with it, it is quite dead." (James 2:14–17)

Conscience

Week 6 ◇ Monday

Yesterday we talked about action and behavior as the proof of loving beyond thoughts, words and feelings. A person can be said to be living a "moral" life if he or she is really trying to put love (and all that that word encompasses) into practice. Immorality is basically a refusal to care about others or selfishness. This selfishness can take the form of unloving sexual behavior or dishonesty in business dealings, but it has a thousand other faces too. Failure to share one's material goods or failure to communicate with one's family is also basically immoral.

This brings us to a discussion of conscience. Conscience, many small children are taught, is the little voice within us pointing out right from wrong. Guilt is its by-product when we have chosen a wrong attitude or action. As we mature, our understanding of conscience also needs to mature. A more adult way to understand this psychological/spiritual dimension of our personalities is to think of conscience as a developed sensitivity or a willing awareness. It means that we keep ourselves open to ourselves and allow the message of love in the Gospel to flood our entire being. It means that we keep before our mind's eye the command of Jesus to love our neighbor as ourselves. We choose not to block this commandment from our conscious awareness and thereby develop a mature Christian conscience. It means that we allow the needs of others to touch us.

An emotionally healthy conscience is to be distinguished from "scrupulosity" which means that we minutely critique every word we utter and every step we take. That only leads to useless anxiety and preoccupation with self-performance, not with the needs of humanity. No, a mature Christian conscience means that we try to see the world with the eyes of Jesus Christ and keep alive within us an attitude of compassion and gentleness. This is what it means to live a moral life.

To Do:

Tonight, before you go to bed, reflect for five minutes about *your* daily patterns within your home and see if there is any small way in which you can attempt to be a more loving person in the future.

Good News for Today:

"You are God's chosen race, his saints; he loves you, and you should be clothed in sincere compassion, in kindness and humility, gentleness and patience. Bear with one another; forgive each other as soon as a quarrel begins. The Lord has forgiven you; now you must do the same. Over all these clothes, to keep them together and complete them, put on love." (Colossians 3:12–14)

What Is Sin?

Week 6 ◇ Tuesday

The understanding of morality we have explored during the last two days we can summarize as loving behavior. To relate the word "sin" to this approach to morality we can go back to the original Greek meaning of the verb "to sin" which is "to miss the mark." This translation might throw a whole new light for you on this word. As a child you probably had an idea of sin as a bad action or a black mark on your soul, or even something associated with purity, sexuality, and "unclean" language. But as in so many other aspects of religion that you began to explore on your retreat and are continuing to explore in this book, it is probably time for you to mature in your understanding of sin.

To miss the mark can be said also in this way: not to be your *best* self. When we look at sin in this general way we can equate it with our discussion of moral behavior. To love is a constant struggle, and many times we fail to act in the most loving way that we should because of our own laziness or selfishness or psychological weakness. We "miss the mark" of doing the loving thing; we fail to be the best self we can be. In no way does this approach to sin minimize our wrong-doing. Sin is definitely a failure or refusal to love. But what it does do is keep the focus on our behavior and upon our struggle to be good people. It doesn't say that because we've sinned *we* are bad (as you may have equated the two as a child). Therefore a good self-image is compatible with the daily struggle to grow and love in spite of the fact that we fail so often.

To Do:

Reflect upon some ways that you are failing to be your best self in your daily life. Allow this material to surface in your awareness and promise yourself an attempt at changing just one small aspect of your behavior patterns.

Good News for Today:

"You must *aim* to be saintly and religious, filled with faith and love, patient and gentle. Fight the good fight of faith and win for yourself the eternal life to which you were called." (1 Timothy 6:11-12)

Mortal and Venial Sin

Week 6 ◇ Wednesday

Sin is such an abstract reality that it is impossible to categorize it. And yet, for the sake of understanding a "moral" life more clearly, we shall attempt to explain different types of sin today and tomorrow. As children your parents probably studied a catechism which talked about "mortal," or serious sin, and venial, or not so serious sin. At one time it almost seemed as though we could have a cookbook list of mortal sins (like murder, adultery and rape) and venial sins (like using profane language and petty theft). Today we in the Church feel that this attempt to categorize types of sins really isn't very smart or very useful, because every bad action is also performed by a person whose heart has to be searched to know the degree of sinfulness, if any at all.

People who ponder such matters in the Church are called theologians. Theologians today talk about sin as the refusal to love—or (as we have discussed) not being the persons we can be. They tend to look upon sin not so much as a specific act (as the old catechism did) but as the "drift" or patterns of a person's life. For example, a husband who neglects his relationship with his wife over a long period of time, who neglects to communicate and share with her, may eventually become sexually involved with another woman (adultery). And so it is the whole drift this man's life has taken away from his wife which is the sin. "Mortal" sin or extremely serious sin according to contemporary theologians is when the wrong one does becomes so much a part of the person's life that it affects their entire being and they turn away from God.

To Do:

"Drifts" often occur unconsciously because people fail to use their consciences and reflect on their behavior lest they have to change. Think for a few moments about your own life. Is there any pattern (like yelling at a younger brother or sister perhaps) which deep down you know isn't right that has become a part of your daily method of operation? And do you feel you could change it?

Good News for Today:

"For a man's words flow out of what fills his heart." (Matthew 12:34)

══════════════════ More Types of Sin

Week 6 ◇ Thursday

There was a song from the musical "Hair" with the line: "Easy to be hard, easy to say no." Another way to look at sin is by seeing it as saying "no." Since sins are actions we talk about "committing" sins. But another perspective and perhaps a more significant one is to look at sin as "omitting" something, as refusing to do a good we could do, as a failure to love. For example, it isn't only sinful to rob a poor person; it is sinful for affluent people never to think or care about a poor person and never to lift a finger to help even one. And so we are talking about sins of "omission" in addition to seeing sin as "commission."

Another viewpoint akin to omission is to look at sin as "submission." By this we mean the unreflective tendency to conform to the norms of our peer culture, our national values and the mores of our society. Some people seem to live like robots, always going along with whatever "the crowd" thinks and does. This refusal to take personal responsibility for our lifestyle and to make choices every day about what is right and wrong is another way to think about sinfulness.

Still another category is sins of "transmission." By this we mean that what we choose to do in this complex society (which food we eat, what products we buy, how we invest our money, how we participate in government) has effects on people all over the world. While we cannot be expected to master the complexities of world economics, on the other hand we cannot ignore our connectedness to other people in this world.

To Do:

Think for a moment about sin as refusal. We all have our "no" word, our method of staying uninvolved. What's your "no" word?

Good News for Today:

"I tell you solemnly, insofar as you neglected to do this to one of the least of these, you neglected to do it to me." (Matthew 25:45)

Week 6 ◊ Friday

We are realizing more and more not only in our personal lives but in our collective lives as well, or in the structures of our society. For example, in the early days of our country slavery was a very common practice in the south. Many slaves were Christians and many slavemasters were also Christian. Slavery to many of them seemed very appropriate as long as the slaves were treated kindly. Of course today we look back and say that that society was caught in a sinful structure without perhaps being too aware of it. We say "sinful" because the very idea of slavery goes against one of the basic tenets of Jesus Christ: that we are all equals in God's eyes. This equality and dignity which each person deserves is called "justice." And so we would say that any structure which is unjust is sinful or morally wrong, and this is a structure which puts people as people in superior and inferior positions.

One sinful structure is racism which says that the color of one's skin determines who is superior and who is inferior in our society. Another is sexism which says that either males or females are superior to the opposite sex. Other sinful structures are any which put down minority groups based on things such as the nationality of people, the religion of people, the sexual orientation of people and so forth. And so it is that when we "examine our consciences" to see if we have sinned or refused to love in our personal lives, we *also* need to ask ourselves if we are a part of any sinful structures in our society. And do we contribute to this structure by putting down any group of people or by the fact that we are silent and don't scream out against injustice?

To Do:

Sometimes within our homes or schools or circle of friends we invent little structures which more or less implicitly say that we are superior and deserve superior treatment and that somebody else is inferior and deserves inferior treatment. Many times this is a very subtle, even close to unconscious, thing we do. Examine your own life for a moment, asking yourself if you are caught up in the web of any unjust patterns of behavior.

Good News for Today:

"All baptized in Christ, you have all clothed yourselves in Christ, and there are no more distinctions between Jew and Greek, slave and free, male and female, but all of you are one in Christ Jesus." (Galatians 3:28)

Coping with Guilt

Week 6 ◊ Saturday

It has been necessary to look at the darker side of morality in our reflections about sin. The last side of that reality we need to focus on is guilt. Guilt is the product of our conscience; it flows from our sensitivity to our failures to be kind and loving. Guilt is often characterized by a type of low-grade depression feeling, a feeling which carries a dislike for our sinfulness and sometimes even an intense dislike of ourselves.

The first thing we need to understand about guilt is that feelings have no morality; they are neither good nor bad. A sexual feeling, an angry feeling, a "fed up with" somebody *feeling,* is not wrong to have. The right or wrong only comes in when we give expression to our feelings because sometimes we express them appropriately and sometimes we don't. But we can't help having feelings; it's our human nature, and so we should never feel guilty about just having them.

A second thing we shouldn't feel guilty about is the appropriate expression of anger. A lot of us get the idea as little children that somehow it's wrong to be angry. That isn't so. Anger is not a bad emotion; it is a very healthy one and *needs* to be expressed. In fact, if we don't express it we take it all within ourselves and bury it and this results in a very unhealthy depression. So when we have a good reason to be angry at someone we really should express it verbally. We haven't the right to use abusive language or abuse someone physically, but we do have the right to let our anger out. Anger isn't appropriate if it *isn't* deserved, however. For instance, if you were out too late and are tired and cranky, it doesn't mean that you have the right to snap at your mother, because it isn't deserved. But deserved anger is not a reason to feel guilty. Even if we choose not to give expression to legitimate anger, we should at least admit to ourselves that we are angry.

If we sin and act unlovingly, it is healthy for us to feel some remorse, some shame, some irritation with ourselves. Why is it healthy? Because out of these feelings come resolutions to change or repair our behavior, and hence the struggle for growth is continued. This is healthy guilt, and we should allow ourselves to feel it. However, guilt becomes unhealthy when we choose to wallow in these emotions and get depressed and feel a lot of self-hatred. This is very unhealthy because first of all we are doing *another* unloving thing by not loving ourselves and being gentle with our growth process. Secondly, to indulge in these feelings often is a substitute for making concrete resolutions and steps to change our behavior. And so to continue to *feel* guilty is unhealthy and gets us nowhere.

To Do:

Ask yourself how long you allow yourself to feel "lousy" about yourself after you have done something wrong. A short period of time is healthy; a long one is not.

71

Good News for Today:

"Jesus then went into the temple and drove out all those who were selling and buying there; he upset the tables of the money changers and the chairs of those who were selling pigeons." (Matthew 21:12)

The First Commandment

Week 7 ◊ Sunday

*I Am The Lord, Thy God. Thou Shalt Not
Have Strange Gods Before Me.*

From the time of the Jews, people have had all sorts of false gods which they believe exist, either in some aspect of nature (like the sun) or in some man-made statue or image. God, through Moses, in his first Commandment, tried to tell the Jewish people that the true God was invisible whereas God in nature could be observed, as could the graven image. And so it took a new jump of faith for a person in Jewish times to be able to believe in an invisible deity.

For us today this commandment remains very significant. We are not prone to look for security by worshiping a graven image. We do, however, look for security where we should not. Many of us look to money and the accumulation of material goods as the number one priority in our lives. Still others of us look to some particular achievement like getting into a particular school or getting a certain position in our company or getting a certain type of status in our community as that which is deserving of *all* our energy. "Strange gods" can also exist in the form of a desire for power or adventure or physical prowess. A person whom we make into a "god" (or a group of persons) to whom we surrender *all* our devotion can qualify as idolatry. And so the point of this Commandment is that the Lord and our relationship with him is the first priority in our lives, and all other relationships and pursuits and goals are secondary to it.

To Do:

List for yourself on a piece of paper a few of your own "false gods."

Good News for Today:

"No servant can be the slave of two masters: he will either hate the first and love the second, or treat the first with respect and the second with scorn. You cannot be the slave both of God and of money." (Luke 16:13)

═══ The Second Commandment

Week 7 ◇ Monday

*Thou Shalt Not Take The Name
Of The Lord Thy God In Vain.*

This Commandment has often been interpreted with respect to swearing. When we swear we usually take something sacred like sexuality or something pertaining to religion and we reduce it to a very low and degrading place. This often helps us, we feel, to express our frustration in the face of something which has happened to us. Swearing is not such a terrible phenomenon, and this Commandment is really not so much against swearing. Let us state first of all that we would not take the name of someone we love and toss it about for ridicule. This is quite clear in young children when someone attacks the mother of one of the children and they react to that injury and feel angry and hurt because someone dear and sacred to them has had her name attacked. So, too, is it with the name of Jesus. The more we grow in the love of Jesus, the less comfortable we will feel using his name in order to express frustration which results in swearing. But even if we do, it is not gravely sinful and probably not even sinful at all. To take the name of the Lord in vain means, really, to insult God totally, to say something really negative about God and really mean it. This Commandment can also be broken by wishing evil upon someone, such as wishing him or her to be damned. Now it is true that we use the words "damn" and "hell" very often with respect to people. For instance, we may tell somebody to go to hell. But we don't really mean it. We just are trying to say, "Get lost," or "You're wrong about that." But if we did really mean a strong insult to someone, if we really did intend to hurt another person intensely by our words, then we would be breaking the second Commandment because, while we wouldn't be taking God's name in vain, we would be taking the name of one of his beloved children on earth, and this would offend him as much as if we said something as angrily against him.

To Do:

Think about a word that has become a part of your vocabulary which might be hurtful or offensive to some other people.

Good News for Today:

"Think how a small flame can set fire to a huge forest; the tongue is a flame like that." (James 3:5)

The Third Commandment

Week 7 ◇ Tuesday

Remember To Keep Holy The Sabbath Day.

This Commandment means a couple of things. First of all, it means that we should worship together with the community on Sunday. A lot of people today throw around the term "Sunday Catholic." A "Sunday Catholic" is a person who just goes to Mass on Sunday but then does not live a loving, Christian life the rest of the week. And it is true that there are some Catholics who do just that. The reason that they go to Mass is out of guilt or out of training from childhood or out of fear of hell. Those are certainly not very good motivations. And one wonders if a person like that really benefits from attending Mass. But just because there are people who are not properly motivated by this law, it does not mean that the law is bad. In human society, when you try to form a community, you have to make compromises. And so, in the Christian community, one day of the week had to be chosen so that all people could arrange their schedules in such a way as to make that a day when they would be available for worship. If we were to say, "Sunday Mass obligation could be replaced by any day of the week," the problem with that would be that not everybody could make it on the same day. As we have it now, most people don't have to work on Sunday, which is a result of the Christian influence upon our nation, and this makes it possible for people to be free to worship together as a community. It often seems that the kids who are opposed to Sunday Mass obligation aren't really experiencing community at Mass, and that's more the problem than the law requiring attendance. One should bear in mind that there are reasonable exceptions to this rule. If a person is ill or doing extensive traveling or some serious matter intervenes on Sunday morning, then we are not obliged to attend Mass. Nor should we forget the story of the man in the Gospel who had something in his heart against his brother and who Jesus said should first go reconcile himself with his brother before he went to offer his gift at the altar. And so neither should we go to worship with the community if there are serious divisions in our life between us and our family or friends. To put it more simply, we should make sure that we are on good terms with other people in a horizontal way before we go to worship God our Father in a vertical way.

To Do:

Go to a Mass this week in addition to Sunday.

Good News for Today:

"So then, if you are bringing your offering to the altar and there remember that your brother has something against you, leave your offering there before the altar, go and be reconciled with your brother first, and then come back and present your offering." (Matthew 5:24)

═══ The Fourth Commandment

Week 7 ◊ Wednesday

Honor Thy Father And Thy Mother.

This is an interesting Commandment for a teenager. Teenagers are often going through a period of reluctance to leave the safety of the home while experiencing the desire for

freedom and autonomy as an emerging young adult. Because of these psychological dilemmas, oftentimes relationships with parents become a little problematic. Parents, for their part, are trying to get used to a child who is growing older and also to try to help the young adult emerge in freedom gradually and not all at once. Parents do this because they know that youths who are given total freedom immediately often suffer because of it. And so this tension makes this Commandment something worthy of our focus. The best way to keep this Commandment is to keep the channels of communication open, to be truthful with parents, not to become deceitful, and to try, as hard as it is, to keep the lines of dialogue open over issues which might be a source of irritation to you. Of course parents have an obligation to honor their children as well, which is the flip side of the same Commandment. And so I would encourage you to do your best to be as open as you can be with your parents about what is going on in your life and to try to level with them as realistically as possible about how you feel. Another thing that is demanded in this Commandment is the following: teenagers in our society often get the idea that because peer relationships are more fun and interesting, the family can be dropped or, in a way, forgotten. This is really not fair to parents who have invested so much love and energy and time and financial resources in their children. It hurts them very much when their teenage children refuse to be present for meals or family gatherings or outings or visits to grandmother and so forth. As teenagers you need to be more sensitive to the feelings of parents, and you need to realize that you are not the only people with feelings. You're not the only age category who can be hurt. By including parents in your life, you are honoring your father and your mother. For those of you who have divorced or separated parents, your honor could take the form of trying to treat each of them with respect and love and not using one parent against the other in order to get some of the things that you want. This would include an attempt to be fair with them, an attempt to be objective about their own conflict between themselves, and also, again, to be aware that parents have feelings too.

Brian Haggarty makes an interesting point in his book *Out of the House of Slavery,* which is an attempt to make the Ten Commandments intelligible to the modern person. He speaks of the fourth Commandment as primarily referring to the treatment of the elderly in American society. How much joy do we bring to a person's day by visiting him or her in a nursing home or by stopping by to say hello on our way from school? How often do we think only of our own selfish pleasure instead of sharing our time, one of the precious commodities, with people who need a little lift? And what about grandparents and elderly aunts and uncles? Maybe we could examine our consciences to see how faithful we are in visiting them, in calling them, in sending them cards, in just thinking about them and praying for their needs.

To Do:

Go out of your way this week to visit an elderly or hospitalized person.

Good News for Today:

"Lord, when did we see you hungry or thirsty, a stranger or naked, sick or in prison, and did not come to your help?" (Matthew 24:44)

The Fifth Commandment

Week 7 ◇ Thursday

Thou Shalt Not Kill.

Today's society is in a unique position as it faces constantly the threat of total human immolation by nuclear disaster. One of the primary questions of conscience a young man or woman must deal with today is: Can I as an adult support the spending of money for defense? Do I believe in escalating defenses of a nuclear nature? If I am opposed to war, what am I doing to live out my opposition? Am I just passive in my objective, in other words? If I am drafted will I refuse to participate in the potential destruction of other human beings? These are serious questions of conscience, and perhaps clarification would be better arrived at if a religious counselor (like a priest or a leader of your youth group) were consulted in order to talk over this serious matter.

Another way to look at this Commandment is to say, "Yes, it is saying that murder is wrong." In the ancient Jewish times, murder was committed without much forethought, it seems. However, there are other ways to kill than with a gun. We can kill with a glance, with a word, with a cutting remark. And so too this Commandment asks us to think about our treatment of others, especially those who are different from us, those whom we might be prone to pick upon. It also asks us to examine the treatment of members within our family where we all know too well each other's points of weakness and vulnerability. Do we take advantage of one another and, in a sense, "kill" each other instead of producing deeper and happier family life?

To Do:

"Think about the last time you "killed" someone by a cutting remark, a laugh or a glance.

Good News for Today:

"Far from passing judgments on each other, therefore, you should make up your mind never to be the cause of your brother tripping or falling. . . . So let us adopt any custom that leads to peace and our mutual improvement." (Romans 14:13, 19)

The Sixth Commandment
Week 7 ◇ Friday

Thou Shalt Not Commit Adultery.

The sixth Commandment literally means that a married person should not have sexual relations with another person. Marriage, from a Christian point of view, is a commitment to another human being. So one way in which we can break the sixth Commandment is by having sexual relations outside of our marriage. But it also has some meaning for those of us who are not married. Implicit in this Commandment is that sexual relations before marriage are not looked upon favorably by the Catholic Church. Now the Church doesn't make this rule just to make life more difficult for teenagers who are feeling their sexual energy in a very strong way. Sin, by one definition, is doing something which ultimately hurts yourself, or, put another way, sin is not being your best self. The Church, in its wisdom, that is to say, the community of believers over the ages, realizes that young people are simply not ready to make the commitment to another person which is intertwined with the act of sexual intercourse. No matter how you slice it, once you have sex in a relationship (as some of you know), the relationship changes. There is just something different about it from that point on. Some of you also may realize that the more sexually intimate we are with a person the more our level of commitment grows. Most people in their teenage years are just not ready for that kind of lifelong commitment. Also much sexual activity among young people is manipulative and, perhaps, relates more to the fifth Commandment where we talked about not hurting or using other people.

To Do:

Just say a prayer today that God will give you the strength to act as you know you should in all your relationships, particularly where there is a romantic involvement.

Good News for Today:

"My grace is enough for you: my power is at its best in weakness." (2 Corinthians 12:9)

═══ **Commandments Seven to Ten**

Week 7 ◊ Saturday

Thou Shalt Not Steal.

To steal means taking what rightfully belongs to another. Cheating on tests and copying of homework certainly would fall under the category of this Commandment, as would justifying the using or the taking of property to which one is not entitled. It is a Commandment that is rather clear and self-evident in its meaning.

Thou Shall Not Bear False Witness Against Thy Neighbor.

This Commandment means simply that we shouldn't lie, that we shouldn't tell untruths. In our current world where we have begun to recognize the importance of psychology, we will also add that the flip side of this Commandment is that we should be honest: honest about ourselves with our friends, honest about our feelings in our relationships with other people, with our peers in school. We all know how important it is to have a good self-image in order to be happy. If we can't be honest with other people about our true selves, we will never have the experience of being accepted as our true selves. And so it is that this Commandment is a very challenging one indeed.

Thou Shalt Not Covet Thy Neighbor's Wife.

This Commandment is somewhat like the sixth Commandment and it means that we should not seek to seduce a person who is in another marriage or, in the case of teenagers, in another happy relationship. To put it more simply, you shouldn't break up other relationships, whether they are male and male, female and female or male and female. We shouldn't try to destroy them out of our own need or impoverishment. We should not be so jealous of other people that we have to have exactly what they have in terms of relationships. We should be happy to become ourselves and to develop our own network of friends without always trying to win people to us who may not be so inclined. We're all too good to get into that sort of thing. And so, basically, this Commandment means that we should try to get rid of envy and jealousy in our life. Of course, *feelings* of jealousy and envy are something that all human beings have and we just don't seem to be able to get rid of them. But this Commandment means that we should recognize these feelings for what they are and learn not to act them out.

Thou Shalt Not Covet Thy Neighbor's Goods.

Again, we are talking about jealousy and envy. The word "covet" means to desire in a way that we shouldn't. And so this Commandment is saying that we shouldn't be jealous of the material blessings of other people or of their particular musical talent or intellectual capacity or athletic prowess. Rather, we should learn to accept ourselves and to be happy with ourselves and to praise God every day for all the blessings that he has given individually to us.

To Do:

Try to "own up" within yourself to someone or something of which you are jealous or envious.

Good News for Today:

"There must be no competition among you, no conceit; but everybody is to be self-effacing. Always consider the other person to be better than yourself, so that nobody thinks of his own interests first but everybody thinks of other people's interests instead." (Philippians 2:3–4)

84

Week 8 ◇ Sunday

Today we will talk about the phenomenon of death and its attendant anxieties. All during this week we will be focusing on various sorts of issues which cause anxiety in young people. Death is of course the fundamental anxiety for every human being at every age in life. If death is meaningless and there is nothing beyond the grave, then life itself is meaningless. This is the concept expanded upon by the existentialist philosophers. The Christian philosophy is that since life does go beyond the grave, life in this world and how we choose to live it is *very* meaningful.

But just because we believe in an afterlife doesn't take away fear of dying for a Christian. It is such a radical change thrusting us into a new mode of existence that we don't know what to expect. It is a new stage of living about which we know so little. It requires a great deal of trust in God to go gracefully into our own death or to deal with the death of people close to us, especially our parents. We can only prepare for death by learning to trust in the Lord's care of us in all the details of our daily living. By reflecting often upon his love for us and by developing the habit of "consulting" with him in prayer we learn gradually how to trust him over our lifetime. And it is simply this trust and nothing else which will give us the courage and spirit of surrender when we eventually confront death in our own lives.

To Do:

Reflecting upon death is not a morbid idea: it can be a very healthy one. There once was a group of monks, and each one used to dig one small shovelful of his own grave each day to remind him of the ending of this stage of life as we know it. Keeping the perspective that we will die someday helps us to appreciate the present and keep the proper priorities in life. What is it like for you to think about your own human frailty? Give that some thought today.

Good News for Today:

"Therefore, you too must stand ready because the Son of Man is coming at an hour you do not expect." (Matthew 24:44)

Heaven and Hell

Week 8 ◇ Monday

Yesterday we reflected upon death as the final stage of living. Since the dawn of civilization mankind has pondered the nature of the afterlife. All of that of course is useless speculation. No one has ever returned to tell us just what this next dimension of life is like. We do get the point, however, from the Gospel that in the next realm there is the experience of reward and punishment. In Jesus' time when even the physical universe was difficult to grasp, people understood life after death in very simple terms. For instance, Jesus spoke of hell as a place of fire to symbolize its aspect of suffering. The apostles thought of heaven as a sort of kingdom where Jesus' closest friends would sit at his right, a place of honor.

Today we have grown beyond looking at spiritual realities in a physical way and understand them more as psychological realities. Therefore we read explanations of heaven as the experience of oneness where we will all be close to God and to each other without the painful chore of communication. We also hear hell described not so much as a place of physical torment but, more probably, of psychological torment where people who choose against God and against community will experience their self-afflicted sense of isolation for all eternity. While these psychological explanations may be more satisfying to modern people, we must recognize that they too are very inadequate.

Probably the best focus to have is not so much to speculate on the nature of heaven and hell but to take seriously Jesus' words that the Kingdom of God is not just an afterlife experience but more importantly it is a present reality here and now, a spiritual reality which very much exists. Heaven and hell therefore do not begin after death; they begin here. If we choose to live an unselfish human existence, if we choose to live for ourselves and others in a courageous way, if we choose to grow a little bit each day, then we will begin to experience a taste of that deep happiness and satisfaction which will be ours more fully in heaven. If we choose to ignore God in our life and to ignore other people and walk all over them for our own selfish purposes, we will begin to have a taste of the misery and isolation which is hell. When we were little kids we thought God "sent" us either to heaven or to hell. As we mature we begin to realize that we create our own heavens and hells and in that sense choose our own destinies.

To Do:

Examine your own childhood notions of heaven and hell. Do you feel you have moved beyond a primitive understanding of these realities?

Good News for Today:

"The things no eye has seen and no ear has heard, things beyond the mind of man, all that God has prepared for those who love him." (1 Corinthians 2:9)

LORD, WHY DIDN'T YOU CREATE THE WORLD IN TWO DAYS AND GIVE US FIVE DAYS' REST?

Week 8 ◇ Tuesday

A source of real worry to a lot of us is having to "die" to our own self in one symbolic sense, not a physical sense. We die to ourselves every time we ignore our own selfish instincts and do something or give up something for another person or group. Every time we give up "our way" of doing something or crush an unkind remark within us or put ourselves out for other people's happiness or comfort we are dying to ourselves. A beautiful example of dying to oneself is the mother of young children who is so busy nourishing and caring for her little ones that she doesn't even have a moment to think about herself.

For some reasons we fear this letting go of our own selfishness. It's as though if we gave in or if we did something for someone else we would lose a part of ourselves by clinging to ourselves, or our viewpoints, our own needs and desire, our own comfort and satisfaction. Paradoxically the message of Jesus is that when we give up our self-interest we discover our true selves. When we give to another we recover something more for ourselves. When we behave unselfishly and in a kindly way toward people we discover our true identity. This is indeed a mystery, something beyond our understanding. And yet it is at the heart of Jesus' teaching and life as well as at the core of every major world religion's body of wisdom. Jesus' physical act of dying on the cross so that we might have "life" is the perfect example of the mystery of giving life to others by our little "deaths" to self each day. Rather than fearing this process of self-denial we should learn to practice it often so that it will not frighten us and in order that we might be transformed into our truest selves.

As a footnote to this reflection let us add that death to self is not inconsistent with a good self-image. Neurotic putting oneself down which is the product of a low self-image is unconscious behavior emerging from the wrong notion that we are undeserving, worthless people. Those with a healthy self-image are capable of "death to self" because they can freely put aside their own needs and desires by a *conscious* and *free choice* to put another person's needs or wishes before their own. They don't (or shouldn't) do this one hundred percent of the time because we need to do things for ourselves too. It's a question of freedom and awareness and balance. A person working (especially in a counseling relationship) on getting rid of a low self-image must be careful to distinguish between behavior resulting from that and Christ-like dying to self.

To Do:

Think of one small way within the next twenty-four hours that you can "die" to yourself to bring a little more "life" to another person.

Good News for Today:

"A man can have no greater love than to lay down his life for his friends." (John 15:13)

Fear of the Gospel

Week 8 ◇ Wednesday

At first it seems to be a contradiction to talk about fearing the Gospel. But in a very real sense it can be a very risky adventure to get involved seriously in the New Testament. Why?

Because it calls us to a very challenging way of life. To follow the example and teachings of Jesus Christ is no easy road. To do so will bring us much peace and deep happiness, but along the way it means that we have to change, to be "born again." And to change our behavior or ways of thinking or dealing with people is no easy thing. It's much easier to keep the Gospel confined to a nice book on our coffee table or to a few nice words we hear in church. But to let the word of God get inside us and really affect us can be a scary thing. It is painful to change and spiritually grow. And if we say we really want to become our best selves, then we have to embrace God's words to us contained in the New Testament.

To Do:

Think about how seriously you have taken the little New Testament passages provided for you each day in this book.

Good News for Today:

"To listen to the word and not obey it is like looking at your own features in a mirror and then, after a quick look, going off and immediately forgetting what you looked like." (James 1:23-24)

Sexuality

Week 8 ◊ Thursday

Another real source of anxiety for many young people (and older people too) is the blossoming of their human sexuality. By sexuality we mean the capacity to relate to other human beings and to love them emotionally, physically, and with sexual expression. Because this capacity to be drawn toward others is the most powerful force within us it can often frighten us. We have already learned that this love needs to be expressed in appropriate ways and with moral considerations.

In this reflection we will not discuss the morality of sexual behavior but rather pose a few points which perhaps are sources of anxiety for you. Many young people are afraid that they are not sexually attractive persons (which usually relates to their own self-image). Others are afraid that they cannot control their sexual passions within certain situations. Others are afraid of sexual feelings toward their own sex, fearful of discovering that they may be homosexuals. These fears and many other fears related to sexuality need to be dealt with. Unfortunately many of us are embarrassed to do so since they are of such a personal nature. But if we leave our fears unspoken in this area they will only torment us increasingly. The thing that we need to do is to talk them out with someone: a friend, a trusted adult, a teacher, a counselor. We need to learn that what we experience is felt by many other people and that we can gain some self-understanding by sharing with someone who can help us in this very special and sacred area of our lives. To communicate about our sexual feelings requires a risk, but without such a risk we will probably feel very troubled and isolated.

To Do:

Think about who it is that you would be comfortable with (relatively anyway) discussing your own sexuality.

Good News for Today:

"What God wants is for you all to be holy. He wants you to keep away from fornication and each one of you to know how to use the body that belongs to him in a way that is holy and honorable." (1 Thessalonians 4:3–4)

The Phenomenon of Worry

Week 8 ◇ Friday

One of the most common occurrences in human existence is the whole problem of uncertainty about the future. Because we are unsure we are inclined to worry. Will we get the job? Does she have that illness? Will I ever find someone to marry me? Can I survive out on my own? There are a million scripts. And yet in the Gospel Jesus tell us that we should look at the flowers in the field. They aren't concerned how they will be clothed, and look how beautiful they are. And look at the birds in the air who don't worry about how they will eat, and their heavenly Father cares for them. Is this romantic and naive? Not really. Jesus is not advocating total passivity, where we just sit back and God will take care of us. What he is advocating, however, is that amid our many strivings we need to never forget to trust that God will care about what happens to us. While it is painful to be unsure about the future, God's love is sure, and he will carry us through to safety, even when it means through the experience of safety. This is what the psalmist meant in the Bible when he wrote: "The Lord is my shepherd; there is nothing I shall want." (Ps 22) It is also what Cardinal Newman meant when he wrote in his poem "Pillar of Cloud": "I do not ask to see the distant scene; one step is enough for me."

Psychology today teaches us also about the uselessness and harmfulness of worry. How many ulcers and headaches and every other kind of ache are its by-product! But it isn't so easy just *to stop* worrying. However, a resolution to cease anxiety is not the correct approach. The approach for us Christians who say that God is a Father who cares about us personally is to build up our trust in him by daily prayer and reading the Gospel. We have to learn to keep turning over to him all the problems we are working on with our human effort, all of our problems big and small. By daily bringing our struggles to God in prayer we will gradually develop a deep and lasting confidence in him and will find the phenomenon of worry and anxiety diminishing in our lives.

To Do:

Look up Psalm 23 in the Old Testament and pray it slowly.

Good News for Today:

"Can any of you, for all his worrying, add a single cubit to his span of life? If the smallest things, therefore, are outside of your control, why worry about the rest? . . . There is no need to be afraid, little flock." (Luke 12:25–26, 32)

═══ Fear of the Retreat's Ending

Week 8 ◇ Saturday

As we discussed earlier in the book we hate to see a good thing end. And many of us who go on retreats hate to see the experience end because we have felt so good during it. We have felt closer to Jesus, to our friends and families, and we also feel better about ourselves. And it's hard to walk away from such good feelings.

One main reason for this type of fear is that we somehow think that the good feelings within us are created by external circumstances: the atmosphere, the retreat team, the retreat house, certain talks, etc. And this is just not true. All that these external stimuli have done (because they have been combined in such an intense positive way) is to bring out feelings and possibilities already within us. They haven't *created* anything at all. And while it is easier for our hearts to be moved with all the right surroundings, we need to learn not to rely on those surroundings so dependently that we cannot get in touch with ourselves without them.

And so one of the main purposes of the retreat is to help us see how close we *can* be with Jesus, how open we *can* be with other people, how good we *can* feel about ourselves. And this is the main point of this book. It has been two months now since your retreat experience. We have been attempting to provide daily reflections on the Gospel which lead to prayer which can help you realize all the possibilities that lie within you. During the next months the burden for spiritual self-actualization is going to be put on you more challengingly.

To Do:

Think about what progress you have made or how you have changed in the last two months. It would be good to write a paragraph or two about this.

Good News for Today:

"Know that the Kingdom of God is near." (Luke 21:31)

Conclusion

It has now been two months since your retreat. If you have been faithful to this daily reflection program you have no doubt experienced real spiritual growth and have integrated the retreat experience into your daily life. Hopefully you have maintained some sort of contact with a member or members of the retreat community. Hopefully you have nourished yourself with the Eucharist and daily Scripture reading. Now that you have become familiar with the New Testament you can use it on your own and make a short daily meditation. Following are instructions for reading the New Testament if you do not already know how. As St. James says in his epistle, "You must do what the word tells you and not just listen to it and deceive yourselves." (James 1:22) This is the purpose of meditation—to let God's word soak into us individually and transform our hearts. And all this started back with your retreat and the experience of God's love in a Christian community. May our Lord Jesus continue to strengthen you each day as you seek to understand your own life in the light he sheds upon you.

Postscript: How To Read the New Testament

The term "New Testament" refers to the second part of the Bible, which begins with the birth of Jesus Christ. The first part of the New Testament is called the Gospel, which literally means the "good news" of humankind's salvation by Jesus. There are four versions of the Gospel, written by four writers (called "evangelists"). They are Matthew, Mark, Luke, and John. Therefore a quote from a Gospel begins with the author's name and is followed by the chapter number and then the verse or verses from the chapter. For example, the Gospel of Luke, chapter ten, verses one through five is written: Luke 10:1–5.

After the four versions of the Gospel comes the Acts of the Apostles, the story of the early Christian community. It is abbreviated as Acts. After that comes the "epistles" or various letters of the early apostles to both communities and individuals. The majority of them are written by St. Paul. These are identified by the person or the community to whom they were written—for example, Ephesians 2:12 or Titus 2:15. When more than one epistle is written to the same community it is preceded by a number—for example, 2 Thessalonians 3:17. The epistles *not* written by St. Paul are identified by the authors: James, Peter, John and Jude. The final section of the New Testament is the Book of Revelation which is very symbolic and written about the end of time. It is very difficult to understand without proper guidance.